An Illustrated Price Guide To Collectible
Barbie Dolls

By
Paris, Susan, & Carol Manos

COLLECTOR BOOKS
P.O. Box 3009
Paducah, Kentucky 42001

The current values in this book should be used only as a guide. They are not intended to set prices, which vary from one section of the country to another. Auction prices as well as dealer prices vary greatly and are affected by condition as well as demand. Neither the Author nor the Publisher assumes responsibility for any losses that might be incurred as a result of consulting this guide.

The prices shown in this guide are derived by the authors, wholly independent of Mattel and Mattel has no connection therewith.

This book makes reference to BARBIE® and other identities for various dolls produced by Mattel, Inc. which are trademarks of Mattel. The dolls and packaging illustrated in this book are used with permission.

Additional copies of this book may be ordered from:

COLLECTOR BOOKS
P.O. Box 3009
Paducah, Kentucky 42001

@ $5.95 Add $1.00 for postage and handling.

Copyright: Susan Manos, 1982
ISBN: 0-89145-185-4

Printed by IMAGE GRAPHICS, Paducah, Kentucky

Dedicated to all
Past, Present, & Future
Barbie Doll Lovers

We would like to say Thank You to:

Dwight F. Smith, Caroline Irish,
Jo Ann Holland, Bernice Lelito,
and Agnes Miller

Introduction

By now, we know the Barbie doll has become one of the most single sought-after dolls. However, the Barbie doll family has become equally as collectible. The purpose of this guide is to help collectors identify the Barbie doll and Barbie doll family.

Pricing any item antique or collectible, requires a great deal of study and experience. Rarity, scarcity, demand and condition assist in determining value.

We hope this handbook will help you with your future acquisitions.

Pricing Guide

Pricing in this book is based on mint-in-box (M.I.B.) dolls. This means never removed from original package.

At least 20% of the M.I.B. value is taken off a doll once it has been removed from the original packaging. A mint doll in its original (manufactured) garb, minus box, is 50% less than the M.I.B. value. Pricing beyond this scale is left to the discretion of the individual.

Table of Contents

Barbie Dolls and Female Friends

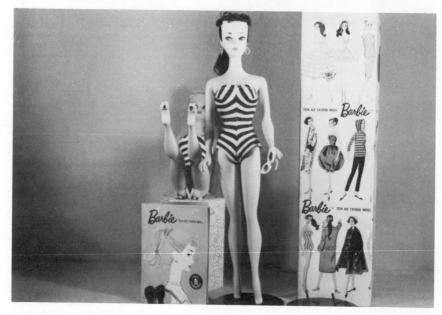

1959 #1 Barbie doll. M.I.B. $700.00. The holes under the #1 Barbie doll's feet are lined with copper tubing.

Close up of 1959 #1 Barbie doll's face.

1959 #2 Barbie doll, blonde, M.I.B. $400.00. 1959 #2 Barbie doll, brunette, M.I.B. $450.00.

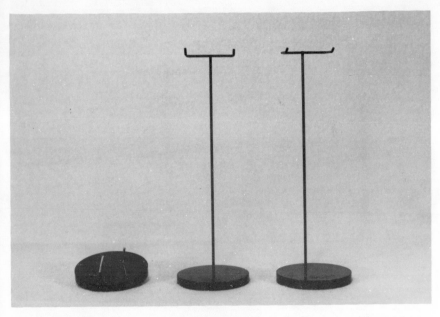

#1 stand, $50.00 and up. #2 stand, $40.00 and up. #3 stand, $30.00 and up.

These rare outfits appeared in the first booklet only. 1959 Easter Parade, M.I.B. $100.00. 1959 Gay Parisienne, M.I.B. $100.00. 1959 Roman Holiday, M.I.B. $100.00.

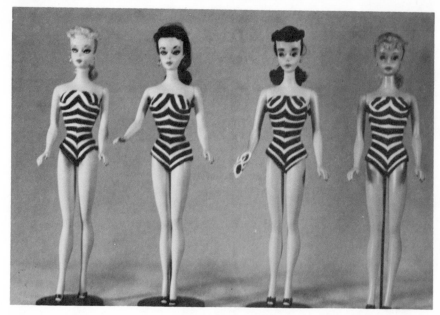

1959 #1 Barbie doll, M.I.B. $700.00. 1951 #2 Barbie doll, M.I.B. $450.00. 1960 #3 Barbie doll, M.I.B. $100.00. 1960 #4 Barbie doll, M.I.B. $75.00.

8

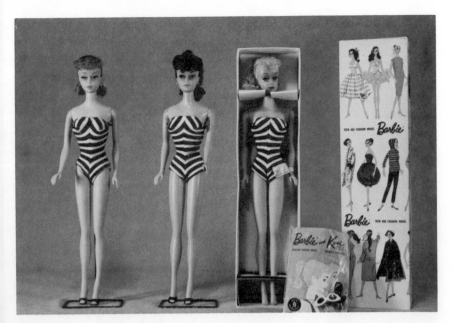

1961, First hollow body Barbie dolls. Often referred to as #5, with three different hair colorings, M.I.B. $60.00 each.

Three different 1962 Bubble cut Barbie dolls, M.I.B. $50.00.

1963 Brunette Midge doll with pink and red suit, M.I.B. $45.00. Midge doll with teeth, also from 1963, M.I.B. $100.00. 1963 Blonde Midge doll with light blue and dark blue suit, M.I.B. $45.00. 1963 Red haired Midge doll with lime green and orange suit, M.I.B. $45.00.

Close-up of 1963 Midge doll with teeth and side glance eyes.

1963 Fashion Queen Barbie doll. Came with three interchangable wigs, M.I.B. $75.00.

1964 "Barbie's Wig Wardrobe," Mint on card $45.00. 1964 "Midge's Wig Wardrobe," Mint on card $75.00. Also shown, Midge doll with molded hair as a put-together doll.

Swirl ponytail Barbie dolls from 1964, brunette, blonde, and redhead, M.I.B. $55.00.

1964 "Miss Barbie" often referred to as "Sleep-eyed Barbie," M.I.B. $300.00. Doll in mint condition with suit, cap and wigs, $150.00 and up.

1965 Bendable Leg Barbie doll with new hair style, short hair with bangs. This style was often referred to as the American Girl style. Blonde and redhead dolls, M.I.B. $50.00. Side-part Barbie doll, hard to find, M.I.B. $150.00. Black haired Barbie doll, also hard to find, M.I.B. $55.00.

Close-up of 1965 side-part bendable leg Barbie doll.

1965 Bendable leg Midge doll, hard to find, M.I.B. $75.00.

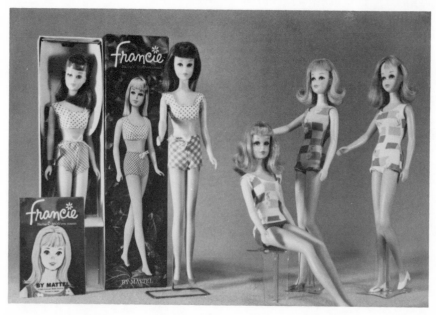

1966 Francie doll, Barbie doll's cousin. Straight leg Francie doll, M.I.B. $40.00. Bendable leg Francie doll, M.I.B. $35.00.

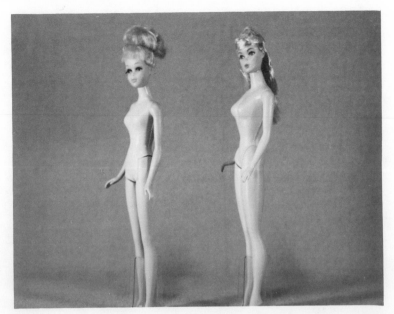

See the reason why the Barbie doll cannot wear the Francie doll's clothes.

1966 Twist 'N Turn Barbie doll, M.I.B. $45.00. 1967 Twist 'N Turn Barbie doll, M.I.B. $45.00. 1968 Twist 'N Turn Barbie doll, M.I.B. $45.00. 1969 Twist Barbie doll, M.I.B. $45.00. 1971 Twist Barbie doll, M.I.B. $45.00.

1967 Black Francie doll. First issue with light brown eyes and red oxidized hair, M.I.B. $160.00. 1967 Black Francie doll. Second issue with darker eyes and dark brown hair, M.I.B. $150.00.

1967 Twiggy, a personality doll. Looks like the Casey doll only hair is shorter and she wears heavier eye make-up, M.I.B. $60.00.

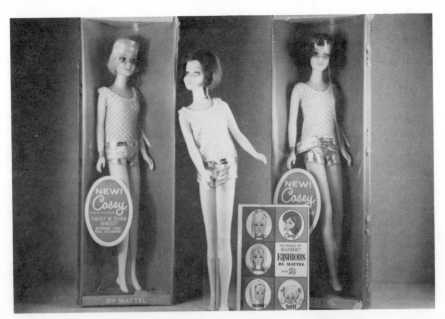

1967 Blonde and brunette Casey dolls, M.I.B. $60.00 each.

1967 Twist 'N Turn Francie doll, M.I.B. $45.00. 1969 Twist 'N Turn Francie doll, M.I.B. $45.00. 1971 Twist 'N Turn Francie doll. Often referred to as "No Bangs Francie". Hard to find, M.I.B. $75.00. 1970 Twist 'N Turn Francie doll, M.I.B. $45.00.

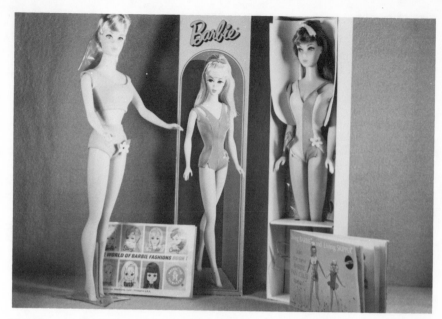

1967 Standard Barbie doll,M.I.B. $35.00. 1970 Standard Barbie doll, M.I.B. $35.00.

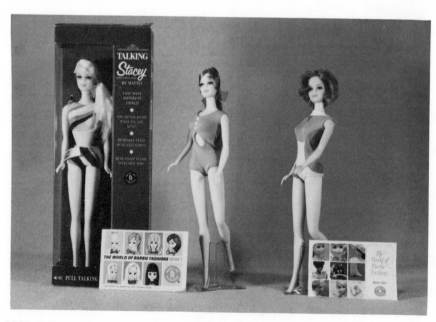

1968 Talking Stacey doll, M.I.B. $40.00. 1968 Twist 'N Turn Stacey doll, M.I.B. $35.00. 1969 New Twist 'N Turn Stacey doll, M.I.B. $40.00.

1969 "New 'N Groovy Talking P.J.," M.I.B. $50.00. 1969 Twist 'N Turn P.J. doll, M.I.B. $45.00.

1968, 1969, and 1971 "Talking Barbie", M.I.B. $50.00 each.

1969 "Talking Truly Scrumptious," M.I.B. $200.00. 1969 Standard Truly Scrumptious doll, M.I.B. $200.00.

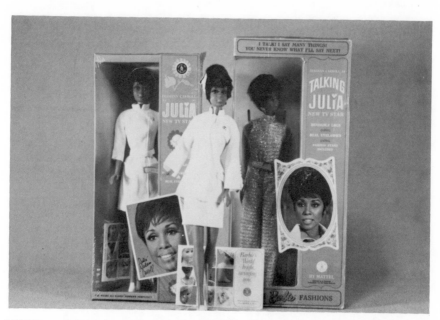

1970 Twist Julia doll, M.I.B. $45.00. 1969 Twist 'N Turn Julia doll in harder to find two piece nurses uniform, M.I.B. $50.00. 1969 Talking Julia doll, M.I.B. $35.00.

1969 New Talking Christie doll, M.I.B. $35.00. 1970 Talking Christie doll, M.I.B. $35.00. 1969 Twist Christie doll, M.I.B. $35.00. 1971 Live Action Christie doll, M.I.B. $50.00.

1970 Barbie doll and Stacey doll display case with four dolls wearing outfits Cloud 9, Winter Wow, Shirtdressy, and Velvet Venture. Mint in case $250.00.

1970 Francie doll, "With Growin' Pretty Hair," M.I.B. $50.00. 1970 Francie doll, "Hair Happenin's," M.I.B. $60.00.

1970 Walking Jamie doll, M.I.B. $60.00. 1970 Walking Jamie doll with dog, part of a Sears gift set. (See gift set chapter).

1969 Living Barbie doll, M.I.B. $45.00. 1971 Dramatic Living Barbie doll, M.I.B. $45.00.

1971 "Live Action Barbie on Stage," M.I.B. $60.00. 1971 "Live Action Barbie," M.I.B. $45.00.

1971 "Live Action P.J. On Stage," M.I.B. $60.00. 1971 "Live Action P.J.," M.I.B. $45.00.

1971 Barbie doll "With Growin' Pretty Hair," M.I.B. $50.00. 1971 Barbie doll "Hair Happenin's," Sears limited edition, very hard to find, M.I.B. $200.00. 1972 Barbie doll "With Growin' Pretty Hair." This doll is harder to find than the 1971 issue, M.I.B. $60.00.

1972 Walk Lively Steffie doll, M.I.B. $60.00. 1972 Walk Lively Barbie doll, M.I.B. $60.00.

1972 "Busy Barbie with Holdin' Hands," M.I.B. $65.00. 1972 "Talking Busy Barbie with Holdin' Hands," M.I.B. $65.00.

1972 "Busy Steffie with Holdin' Hands," M.I.B. $70.00. 1972 "Busy Francie with Holdin' Hands," M.I.B. $70.00. 1972 "Talking Busy Steffie with Holdin' Hands," M.I.B. $70.00.

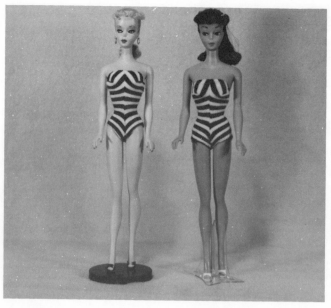

#1 Barbie doll and Ward's Anniversary Barbie doll from 1972. Ward's Anniversary Barbie doll, M.I.B. $100.00.

1971 Malibu Barbie doll. 1972 Malibu P.J. doll. M.I.B. $20.00 each.

1972 Walk Lively "Miss America" doll. Promotional from the Kellogg Co. This doll came in a plain mailing box, M.I.B. $30.00. 1973 Blonde Quick Curl "Miss America" doll offered at most stores, M.I.B. $15.00. 1973 Brunette Quick Curl "Miss America" doll with longer hair and twist waist. This doll is harder to find, M.I.B. $75.00.

1973 Quick Curl Barbie doll with extra outfit. This was a store promotion issue, mint on card $50.00.

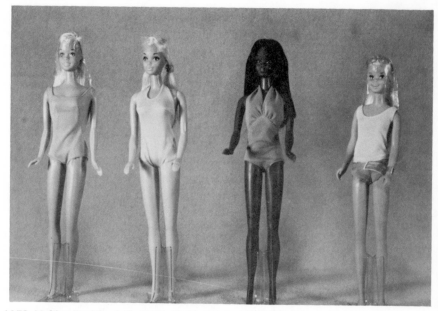

1973 Malibu Barbie doll. 1974 Malibu P.J. doll. 1973 Malibu Christie doll. 1971 Malibu Francie doll. M.I.B. $10.00 each.

1973 Quick Curls. Barbie doll, M.I.B. $30.00. Cara doll, M.I.B. $25.00. Francie doll, M.I.B. $30.00. Kelley doll, M.I.B. $35.00.

1974 Sun Valley Barbie doll, M.I.B. $35.00. 1974 Gold Medal Barbie doll, M.I.B. $20.00. 1974 Gold Medal Skier doll, M.I.B. $25.00.

1974 Barbie doll "Sweet Sixteen," M.I.B. $25.00. 1974 Barbie doll "Sweet Sixteen," with promotional outfit on card, $30.00.

1974 Yellowstone Kelley doll, hard to find, M.I.B. $55.00. 1974 Newport Barbie doll, M.I.B. $45.00.

1975 Free Moving Barbie doll, Cara doll and P.J. doll, M.I.B. $30.00 each.

1975 Baggie Francie doll and Baggie Casey doll. This is the last issue of these dolls to appear on the market. Mint in bag, $15.00.

Quick Curl Francie doll. Limited edition with special costume offer, M.I.B. $45.00.
Twist 'N Turn Barbie doll with extra outfit. Limited edition, M.I.B. $75.00.

1976 Deluxe Quick Curls. Cara doll, M.I.B. $20.00. P.J. doll, M.I.B. $20.00. Barbie
doll, M.I.B. $20.00.

1976 Ballerina Barbie doll. First issue with hair pulled to back of head, M.I.B. $20.00.
1978 Ballerina Barbie doll. Second issue, with heavier eye make-up and side curl added, M.I.B. $15.00. 1976 Ballerina Cara doll in pink tutu, M.I.B. $25.00.

Close-up of 1976 and 1978 Ballerina Barbie dolls.

1976 Ballerina Barbie doll On Tour. This was a department store special. *Not Shown.* M.I.B. $35.00. 1978 re-issue Ballerina Barbie doll On Tour. Three costume variations, sold in selected stores, M.I.B. $25.00.

1976 Beautiful Bride Barbie doll, first issue, a Department Store Special, M.I.B. $35.00.

The Barbie Doll's Male Friends

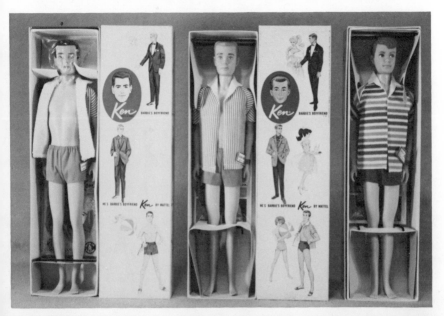

1961 First issue flocked-hair Ken doll came with bathing trunks, sandles and towel. *Not shown.* M.I.B. $65.00. 1961 Second issue Ken doll with flocked hair, M.I.B. $50.00. 1962 Painted hair Ken doll, M.I.B. $45.00. 1963 Allen doll, M.I.B. $45.00.

1964 Bendable leg Ken doll and Bendable leg Allen doll. These dolls are harder to find, M.I.B. $100.00.

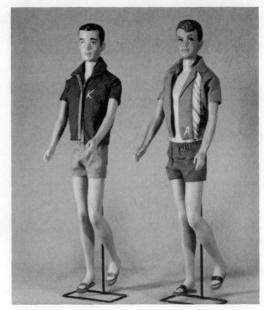

1970 New Talking Brad doll. 1969 Talking Ken doll. M.I.B. $45.00 each.

1971 "Live Action Ken On Stage," M.I.B. $50.00. 1971 "Live Action Ken," M.I.B. $40.00.

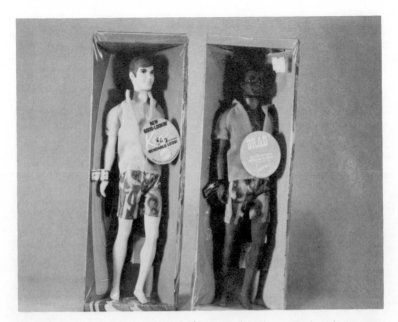

1970 Bendable leg Ken doll, M.I.B. $40.00. 1971 Bendable leg Brad doll, M.I.B. $40.00.

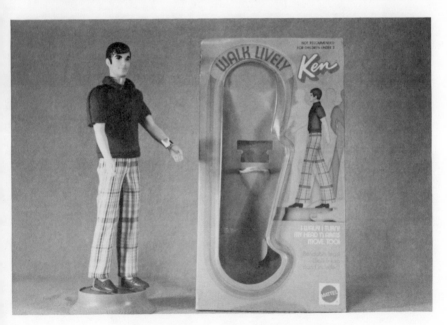

1972 "Walk Lively Ken," M.I.B. $60.00.

1972 Busy Ken doll. 1972 Talking Busy Ken doll. M.I.B. $45.00 each.

1971 Malibu Ken doll, M.I.B. $15.00. 1973 Mod Hair Ken doll, M.I.B. $20.00. 1976
Now Look Ken doll, two versions, M.I.B. $20.00 each.

1975 "Gold Medal Ken Skier," M.I.B. $25.00. 1974 "Sun Valley" Ken doll, M.I.B. $30.00.

1975 Free Moving Ken doll, M.I.B. $20.00. 1975 Free Moving Curtis doll. This doll was only out for one year. Hard to find, M.I.B. $30.00.

The Younger Set

1964 Skipper doll, M.I.B. $40.00. 1965 Skooter doll, M.I.B. $40.00. 1965 Ricky doll, M.I.B. $45.00.

1965 Bendable Leg Skipper doll, M.I.B. $45.00. 1966 Bendable Leg Skooter doll, M.I.B. $45.00.

1966 Tutti doll "Night Night Sleep Tight" play set, M.I.B. $65.00. This set was also re-issued in Europe in 1975, M.I.B. $35.00. *Not shown.* 1966 Tutti doll "Walkin' My Dolly" play set, M.I.B. $65.00. This set was also re-issued in Europe in 1975, M.I.B. $35.00. *Not shown.*

1966 Tutti and Todd dolls "Sundae Treat" play set, M.I.B. $125.00. 1966 Tutti doll "Melody In Pink" play set. Came in two different dress colors, pale pink and hot pink. M.I.B. $75.00 each.

1967 Tutti doll "Cookin Goodies" play set, M.I.B. $75.00. 1966 Tutti doll "Me and My Dog" play set, M.I.B. $125.00. 1975 Re-issued, Tutti doll "Swing-A-Ling," M.I.B. $35.00. 1967 Tutti doll "Swing-A-Ling" play set. *Not shown.* M.I.B. $75.00.

1966 Tutti doll blonde and brunette, M.I.B. $40.00. 1966 Todd doll, hard to find, M.I.B. $45.00. 1967 Chris doll, hard to find, M.I.B. $45.00. 1967 Tutti doll, M.I.B. $30.00. 1969 Tutti doll, M.I.B. $30.00.

1967 Re-issued Bendable leg Skipper doll, rare when M.I.B. only, $65.00. 1968 Twist 'N Turn Skipper doll, M.I.B. $35.00. 1969 New Twist 'N Turn Skipper doll, M.I.B. $35.00. 1970 Twist Skipper doll, M.I.B. $35.00. 1970 "New Living" Skipper doll, M.I.B. $35.00.

1970 Pretty Pairs. Nan 'N Fran dolls, Angie 'N Tangie dolls, Lori 'N Rori dolls, all hard to find, M.I.B. $75.00 each. 1968 Buffy and Mrs. Beasley dolls, M.I.B. $45.00.

1971 Fluff doll, M.I.B. $45.00. 1972 Tiff doll, hard to find, M.I.B. $75.00.

1973 Pose 'N Play Skipper doll, (Baggie), Mint in Bag, $15.00. 1973 "Quick Curl" Skipper doll, M.I.B. $20.00. 1971 Malibu Skipper doll, M.I.B. $15.00.

1975 "Growing Up" Skipper doll, M.I.B. $11.00. 1976 "Growing Up" Ginger doll, M.I.B. $20.00.

European re-issued Tutti doll, Todd doll, Chris doll & Carla doll. Tutti doll, M.I.B. $20.00. Todd doll, M.I.B. $20.00. Chris doll, M.I.B. $20.00. Chris doll, M.I.B. $25.00. Carla doll, M.I.B. $25.00.

Gift Sets and Dressed Box Dolls

Dressed Box Dolls, in marked boxes with blue bands. M.I.B. $125.00 and up.

Barbie doll Sparkling Pink Gift Set, M.I.B. $200.00.

Skipper doll Party Time Gift Set, M.I.B. $125.00.

Living Barbie doll Action Accents Gift Set, Sears Exclusive, M.I.B. $150.00.

Walking Jamie doll, Strollin' In Style Gift Set, Sears Exclusive, M.I.B. $150.00.

Barbie doll Twinkle Town Gift Set, Sears Exclusive, M.I.B. $125.00.

Francie doll Rise 'N Shine Gift Set, Sears Exclusive, M.I.B. $125.00.

Malibu Ken doll, Surf's Up Gift Set, Sears Exclusive, M.I.B. $100.00.

Toys and Accessories

Barbie Photo Album, $15.00. "Barbie Sings" Record Set, $20.00. Barbie Diary, $15.00.

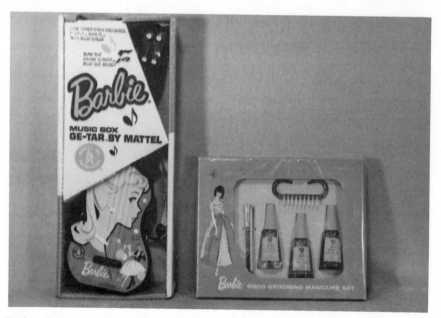

Barbie Music Box GE-TAR, M.I.B. $20.00. Barbie Good Grooming Manicure Set, M.I.B. $25.00.

Barbie Sportscar, M.I.B. $50.00.

Hot Rod, M.I.B. $60.00.

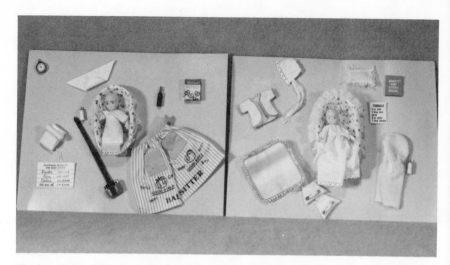

"Barbie Baby Sits" Set (first issue), M.I.B. $100.00. "Barbie Baby Sits" Layette, M.I.B. $125.00. Rare.

"Dog 'N Duds," M.I.B. $100.00. "Dog 'N Duds," Dog only, $20.00.

Barbie and Francie Color Magic Fashion Designer Set, M.I.B. $100.00.

"Barbie's Horse, Dancer," M.I.B. $45.00.

Mattel "Fashion Teeners." Fun to add to a Barbie doll collection. M.I.B. $20.00 each.

Sears Exclusive Boat, M.I.B. $35.00.

Barbie "Hair Fair" Sets, M.I.B. $20.00 each.

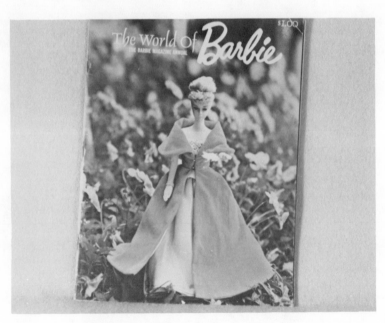

Early Fan Club Magazine, $4.00 each. Later Fan Club Magazines *(Not shown)*, $3.00 each.

Barbie Pool Party Set, M.I.B. $15.00.

"Barbie's Ten Speeder," M.I.B. $10.00. "Barbie Baby-sits," Sears Special, M.I.B. $10.00.

"Barbie Sunsailer," M.I.B. $20.00. "Olympic Gymnast Set," M.I.B. $20.00.

Wrist Watch Wall Clock. Gift from Judy Fryer and Carolyn Mukrdechian.

Structures, Rooms & Furniture

"Barbie's Dream House," shown closed. Complete, $25.00.

"Barbie's Fashion Shop." Complete, $65.00.

"Barbie's New Dream House." Shown closed. Complete, $65.00.

"Barbie's Dream Kitchen-Dinette." Shown closed. Complete, $65.00.

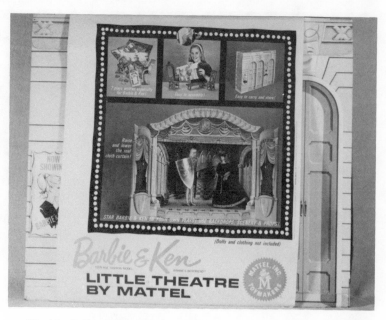

"Barbie & Ken Little Theatre." Shown closed. Complete, $75.00.

"Skipper Dream Room." Shown closed. Complete, $55.00.

"Barbie 'N Skipper Go-together Living Room Furniture Group." M.I.B. $55.00. "Barbie Dining Room Set," M.I.B. $60.00. *Not shown.*

"Barbie Chair, Ottoman, & End Table," M.I.B. $30.00. "Barbie Convertible Sofa-bed & Coffee Table," M.I.B. $40.00.

"Barbie Chaise Lounge & Side Table," M.I.B. $35.00.

"Barbie Lawn Swing & Planter," M.I.B. $85.00.

"Susy Goose, Barbie's Dressing table," M.I.B. $25.00; Wardrobe, M.I.B. $20.00; Bed, hard to find, M.I.B. $40.00.

"Susy Goose Music Box Piano," M.I.B. $100.00.

"Susy Goose, Barbie's Wardrobe," M.I.B. $20.00; Canopy Bed, M.I.B. $25.00; Dressing Table, M.I.B. $25.00.

"Susy Goose Ken Wardrobe," M.I.B. $35.00.

"Susy Goose Skipper Wardrobe," M.I.B. $25.00; Bed, M.I.B. $25.00; Dressing Table, *Not shown*, M.I.B. $30.00.

"Skipper 'N Skooter Bunk Beds and Ladder," M.I.B. $55.00.

"Barbie Cookin' Fun Kitchen," M.I.B. $30.00.

"Barbie Teen Dream Bedroom," M.I.B. $30.00.

"Barbie Lively Livin' Room," M.I.B. $30.00.

"Barbie's Room-fulls." Firelight Living Room, Country Kitchen, Studio Bedroom, M.I.B. $25.00 each.

"Skipper 2-in-1 Bedroom," M.I.B. $35.00.

"Barbie Beauty Bath," M.I.B. $20.00. "Barbie's Bathe'n Beauty Place," Sears Special, M.I.B. $25.00.

Cases

Two early Barbie doll cases, $4.00 each.

Two early Ken doll cases, $4.00 each.

Extra large Barbie and Midge doll case, $6.00.

Unusual hard plastic case, holds four dolls plus wig stand, $12.00.

Two cases from 1965. Note the "Side Part Barbie" on the case on the right. $6.00 each.

Extra large Barbie & Francie doll case, $10.00.

Skipper doll case, $4.00. Skipper and Skooter doll case with see-through window, $4.00.

Double size Skipper and Skooter doll case, $5.00.

Tutti & Chris doll case, Tutti play case, $5.00 each.

Standard size Stacey doll case, $5.00. Six Sided Francie doll case, $6.00.

Booklets

Although these booklets appear in the last chapter, they are considered as important as the Barbie doll herself. They are the greatest source of costume information available.

The top three booklets are dated 1958. #1 featured the 3 rare outfits shown on page 8. $15.00. #2 was the last booklet to feature the Commuter Set. $5.00. #3 was the last booklet to feature the Barbie doll alone on the cover. $5.00. The booklets on the bottom row are deep pink in color, dated 1961, and feature the Ken doll for the first time. $2.00 each.

Top row, left to right: 1962, light blue. 1962, white. 1962, blue. $2.00 each. Bottom row: 1962, yellow. $2.00.

Booklets dated 1963. Book 1, $3.00. Book 2, 3 & 4, $2.00 each.

Booklets dated 1964. Book 1, $3.00. Book 2, 3 & 4, $2.00 each.

These booklets are red in color, dated 1965 and are the hardest series to find. Book 1, $7.00. Book 2, 3 & 4, $5.00 each.

Booklets dated 1966. Book 1, $3.00. Book 2 & 3, $2.00 each.

Booklets dated 1967. Book 1, $2.50. Book 2 & 3, $1.50 each. Bottom right dated 1966, $1.50.

Top row: Booklets dated 1968. Book 1, $1.50. Unnumbered book, $2.00.
Bottom row: Booklet dated 1969, $1.00.

Top row: Booklets dated 1970, $1.00 each. Bottom row: Booklet dated 1971, $2.00.

Top row: Booklet dated 1972, $2.00. Bottom row: Booklet dated 1973, $2.00.

Top row: Skipper booklet, 50¢. Tutti booklet, hard to find, $4.00. Center row: Fashions and Play Accessories booklet, $3.00. Bottom row: Skipper, Skooter & Ricky booklet, $1.00. Francie booklet, hard to find, $4.00.

As Collectors, we predict that the Barbie doll (in the near future) will become the most collectible doll of all time.

We Salute You
Long Live Barbie Dolls
Queen of (Today's) Dolls

About The Authors

Paris - Semi-retired from Chrysler Corp., Amateur Photographer, Co-Promoter of Roma's of Bloomfield Doll Shows and Member of Detroit Doll Collectors Club.

Susan - Proprietor of Susan's Doll Museum, Collector and Appraiser of antique and collectible dolls for 17 years, Author of *Schoenhut Dolls and Toys, A Loving Legacy*, Co-Promoter of Roma's of Bloomfield Doll Shows, and Member of Detroit Doll Collectors Club and Dolls and Friends Club of Royal Oak.

Carol - Junior at Warren Woods High School, Participant in Distributive Education Clubs of America (DECA), Collector of Modern Dolls, and Junior Member of Detroit Doll Collectors Club and Dolls and Friends Club of Royal Oak.